· JOANNA COLE ·

How You Were Born

Revised and Expanded Edition

Photographs by
MARGARET MILLER

Morrow Junior Books / New York

ACKNOWLEDGMENTS

The author wishes to thank Louise Bates Ames,
Anne C. Bernstein, and Dr. David Kliot for reading and
suggesting changes in the manuscript for this book.

The photographer is grateful to the staff and families
at the Maternity Center Association, 48 East 92 Street,
New York City, and especially to Elizabeth Haak,
Director of Public Information, who worked extraordinarily
hard to make this project a success.

Picture credits: Joanna Cole, p. 5; Lennart Nilsson, pp. 12, 15, 23, 24;
Erika Stone/Photo Researchers, p. 46; Arthur Tilley/FPG
International, p. 48. Drawings on pp. 19, 20, 21, 27, and 34
by Ann Neumann.

Library of Congress Cataloging-in-Publication Data
Cole, Joanna. How you were born : illustrated with photographs / by Joanna Cole.
—Rev. ed. p. cm.
Summary: Text and photos explain how a baby is conceived, how it grows
inside the mother's womb, and how it is born.
ISBN 0-688-12059-8 (trade).—ISBN 0-688-12060-1 (library)
1. Embryology, Human—Juvenile literature. [1. Pregnancy.
2. Childbirth. 3. Babies.] I. Title.
QM601.C66 1993 612.6′3—dc20 92-23970 CIP AC

For Rachel

A Note to Parents

It is natural for children to ask "Why?" Just as they are curious about how a telephone works or what snow is made of, children also wonder where they came from and how they were born. When their questions are answered in a natural, open way, they can feel good about themselves and their feelings, trusting in the adults in their life.

One good reason for talking with children about birth is that it shows them that you approve of them and their natural curiosity, and it helps them feel secure. But there is another reason as well, and that is to clear up confusion. Misunderstandings about birth and reproduction are common among children. For instance, having heard that a baby grows in its mother's "tummy," children sometimes worry that the infant is being showered with chunks of pizza or hot soup. The notion of sperm as "seed" engenders many horticultural images. Children may believe that they were planted in the ground or that a woman becomes pregnant by swallowing a seed. The idea of the ovum as an "egg" leads some children to think that they hatched from a chicken's egg or that they were once a baby bird. Some other common misconceptions are that babies are purchased at a store or hospital; that babies are born from the mother's navel, ureter, or anus; and that babies are manufactured, the way a doll might be constructed in a factory.

Ideas like these might seem harmless enough, even charming at first. But for some children they can cause disturbing worries, and a calm explanation of the facts can be reassuring. Because it is not always easy for an adult to predict what inaccurate ideas a child may have, it can help to answer children's questions first with one of your own: "What do you think?" Once you find out what a child is really asking, you'll be in a better position to give a helpful answer based on the facts.

It may be difficult for young children to grasp some concepts, no matter how well or how often they are explained. There is no need to worry about this. Children's view of the world and their capacity to understand keep expanding as they mature, and they need to ask the same questions over again, fitting the information into their new level of understanding.

The biological facts of how babies are born, however, cannot be separated from a child's feelings. A child is interested in hearing the story of her own birth—when it is told in a loving way—because it affirms her parents' love and her own sense of how

much she has grown. Therefore, it is not necessary or desirable to assume a grave or instructional tone. The atmosphere parents wish to create when talking with children about birth and reproduction is a warm, honest, and reassuring one that tells children they are free to ask questions as often as they need to, and you will answer them as lovingly as you know how.

This book was designed to tell children the story of birth in a simple yet informative way. Preschool children often have an avid interest in babies and birth, but may not be ready for a full reading of the text. A partial reading can be just as valuable. You can concentrate on reading what is most interesting to your child, and for the rest of the book, simply talk about what he sees in the pictures.

When my own child was younger, my husband and I read her this book often. We stopped frequently to answer questions, to talk

8

about the pictures, and to compare her own birth, which was by cesarean, with what was described in the book. Children born by cesarean need to know that theirs is simply another way to be born, and that the important parts of birth—the happy expectation of parents and the warm feelings between parents and baby—are the same.

A good time to reminisce about how a child was born is when a new baby is expected. Then a child likes to remember a time when he was the center of attention. Sharing memories about his own birth shows him that he is special to you and can't be displaced in your affections.

As parents and children read together, questions will come up. Many will be easy to answer, but some will not. Sometimes parents feel inadequate when they don't know all the answers. But reproduction is a complicated business, and no one can know everything about anything. The simplest way to handle your own ignorance is to admit it freely, saying "I don't know" or "I'm not sure." If it seems important to answer a question, you can try to find out by consulting other sources. Some books that I have found helpful for getting more information and also in deciding how to word explanations and how much or how little to say to children at various ages are listed at the end of this section.

The youngest children are usually not very interested in knowing how the sperm and ovum get together. But as they grow, they may wonder about this. When children ask, it is best to give simple, straightforward answers and to give only as much information as a child seems to want at the time. The books listed here will be especially helpful with this.

Some parents say that their children do not ask any questions

and are not curious. Probably the children have as much natural curiosity as any, but they may have gotten the impression that birth and reproduction are not something to talk about. If you would like to offer a child the opportunity to ask, you can open things up by saying something like, "Lots of children have questions about how babies are born. If you have any, I'm available to talk about them."

When parents establish this kind of open, caring relationship from an early age, children will have a reliable source of information and guidance to turn to as they grow. My hope is that this book can be a part of that relationship for you and your child.

Joanna Cole

FOR FURTHER READING:

A Child Is Born. Photographs by Lennart Nilsson, text by Lars Hamberger. New York: Delacorte Press, 1990. A classic photographic study of the development in the womb and birth of a baby.

The First Nine Months of Life. By Geraldine Lux Flanagan. New York: Simon and Schuster, 1962. A sensitive description of prenatal development, illustrated with photographs and drawings.

The Flight of the Stork. By Anne C. Bernstein, Ph.D. New York: Dell Publishing Co., Inc., 1980. A child psychologist explains how children at various ages understand birth and advises parents on how to tell children about birth and reproduction.

Being Born. By Sheila Kitzinger, photographs by Lennart Nilsson. New York: Putnam, 1986. A book intended for school-age children and young people, this contains much information on birth that will also be useful to parents.

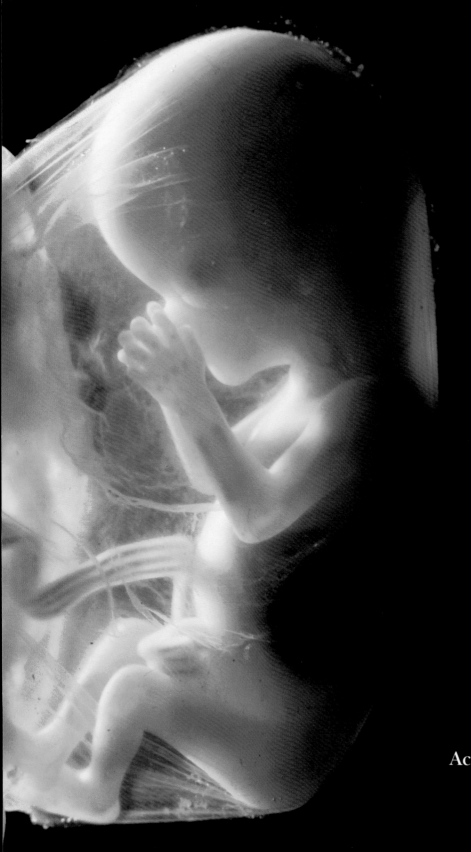

Age: 4 months
Actual size: about 8 inches

Before you were born, you grew in a special place inside your mother's body called her uterus, or womb. There, in a clear sac, you floated in a liquid that was like warm water.

13

Inside the uterus it was dark. You could not see, but you could move, feel, and even hear. You heard your parents' voices talking and the sound of your mother's heart beating.

Perhaps you sucked your thumb sometimes, like the unborn baby in the picture.

Age: 4 months
Actual size: about 8 inches

By the time you were born, you had eyes and ears, a brain and heart, arms and legs, fingers and toes—all the parts you need to live in the world.

But nine months before, when you first began, you were just one little cell, even smaller than the dot at the end of this sentence. Half of this cell came from your mother's body, and the other half came from your father's body.

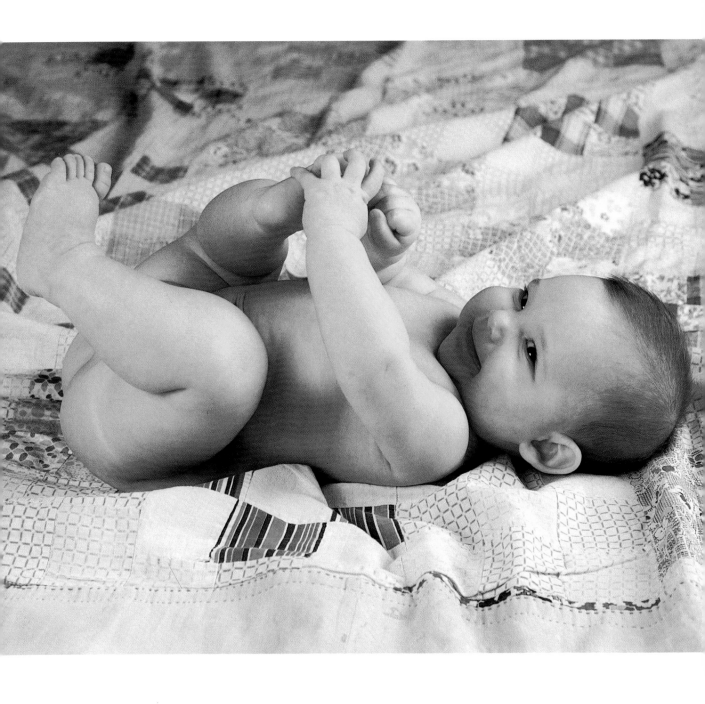

Inside a woman's body and inside a
man's body are tiny cells that can start a
baby. These cells are so small we need a
microscope to see them.

In a woman's body are egg cells. The egg cell is round. It does *not* have a shell like a chicken's egg. In a man's body are sperm cells. The sperm cells have long tails and can swim. When a sperm and an egg join together, they form a special cell that can grow into a baby.

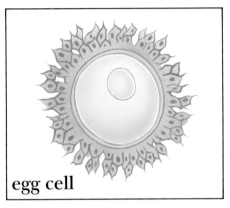

egg cell

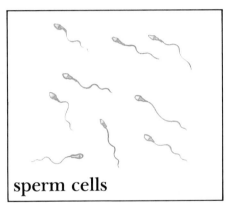

sperm cells

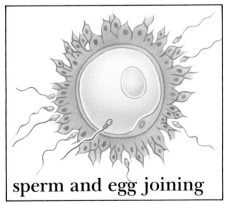

sperm and egg joining

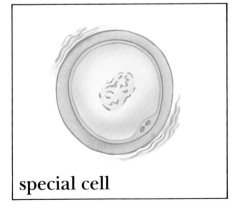

special cell

All cells shown greatly enlarged.

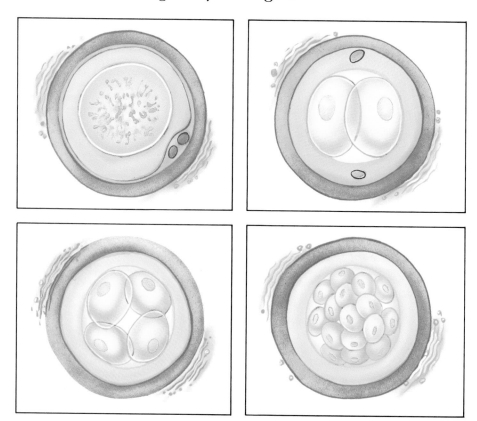

The special cell starts to grow by
dividing, or splitting, to make two cells.
Then each of these cells divides in half
again. Now there are four cells. They
divide again and again. In a short while,
there are hundreds of cells.

After a few weeks of growing, there are millions of cells. They have formed a shape. This shape does not seem much like a baby, but it is the beginning of one. It will look more and more like a baby as it keeps growing.

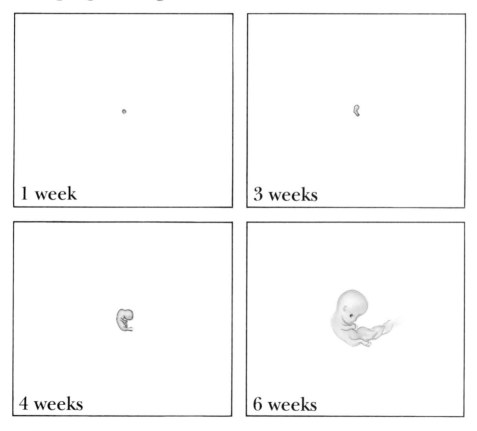

1 week	3 weeks
4 weeks	6 weeks

All above shown actual size.

When you had been in your mother's uterus for about six weeks, your hands and feet had started to grow. Your eyes were there too. They were wide open because your eyelids had not yet formed.

Inside your body, your heart was already beating! In this picture, you can see the red heart inside the unborn baby's chest.

The picture is much larger than the actual size of the unborn baby, which could fit inside a nutshell!

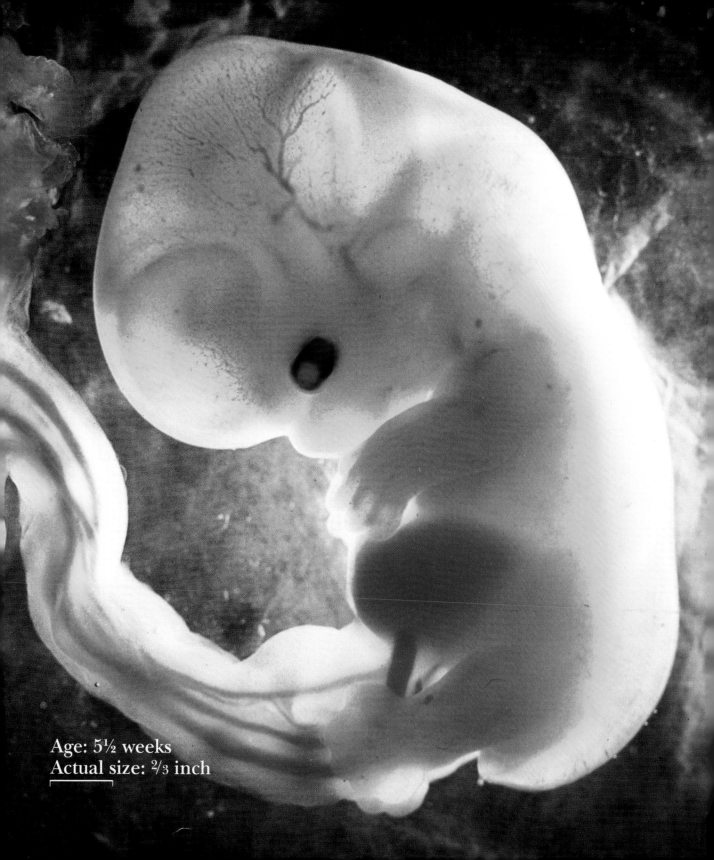

Age: 5½ weeks
Actual size: ⅔ inch

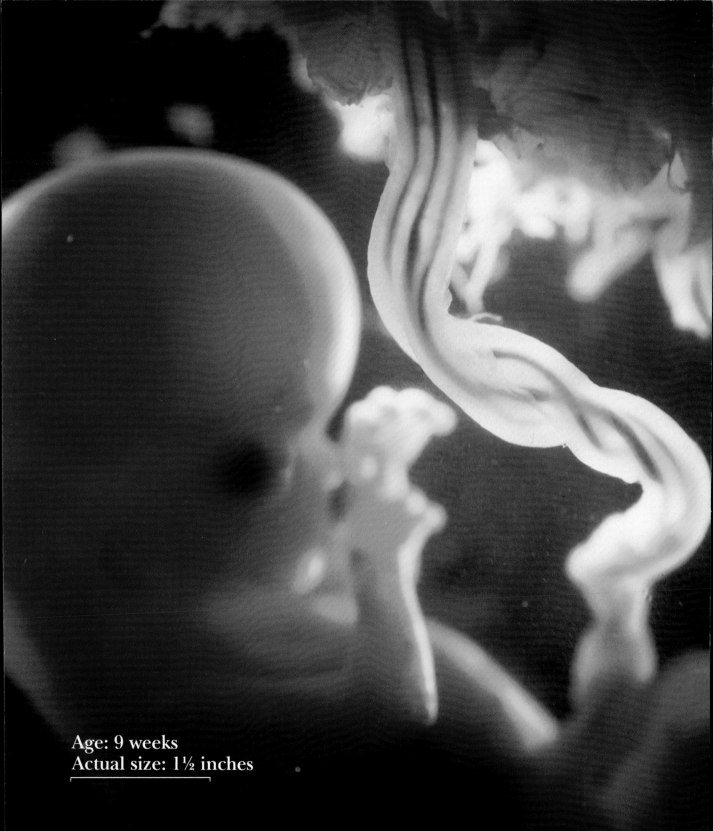

Age: 9 weeks
Actual size: 1½ inches

Already your mother was taking care of you by eating good, nourishing food. Food and oxygen came to you from your mother's body through blood vessels. The blood vessels were inside a tube called the umbilical cord, which was attached to your belly. In the picture, you can see the red blood vessels in the umbilical cord.

Your body wastes were carried away through the blood vessels too. The umbilical cord worked as a kind of two-way transport system.

As your muscles grew, you started moving your arms and legs. Sometimes you turned a complete somersault in the uterus!

During the fourth month, your mother could feel you moving inside her. Soon others could touch her belly and feel you moving too.

As the months went by, you grew bigger and bigger. Your mother's belly had to stretch way out to make room for you.

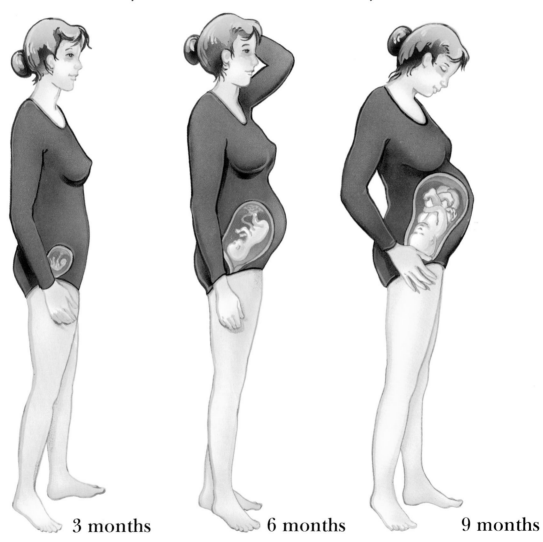

3 months   6 months   9 months

At nine months, you were ready to live outside the uterus. Your mother and father knew you would be born soon, so they started getting ready for you.

One day, your mother felt sharp twinges
called labor pangs. The uterus was
contracting, or squeezing, to push you out
into the world.

Your mother and father went to the hospital or childbirth center where you were to be born. If you were born at home, then the doctor or midwife came to your house.

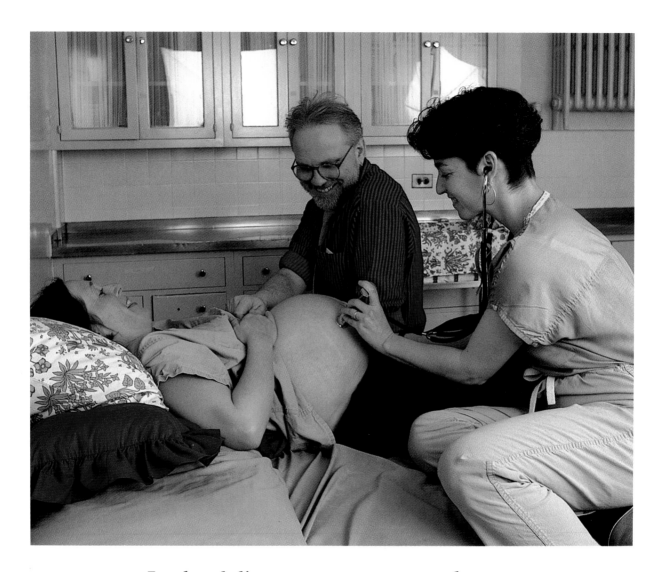

In the delivery room, your mother got
help from your father, from her doctor or
midwife, and from a nurse.

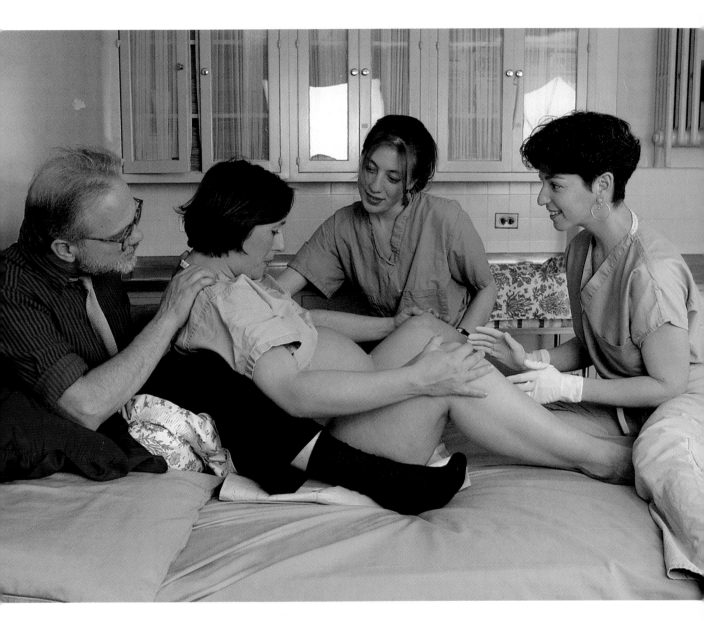

After several hours, you started to be born!

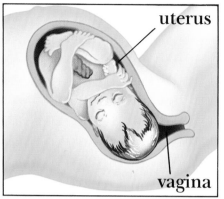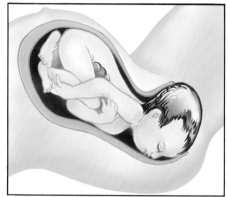

You went from the uterus into the vagina, a special tunnel that connects the uterus to the outside. The vagina can stretch wide to let a baby pass through.

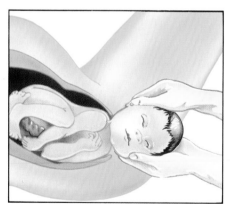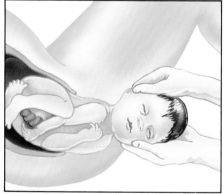

First, your head appeared. Then your whole body came out!

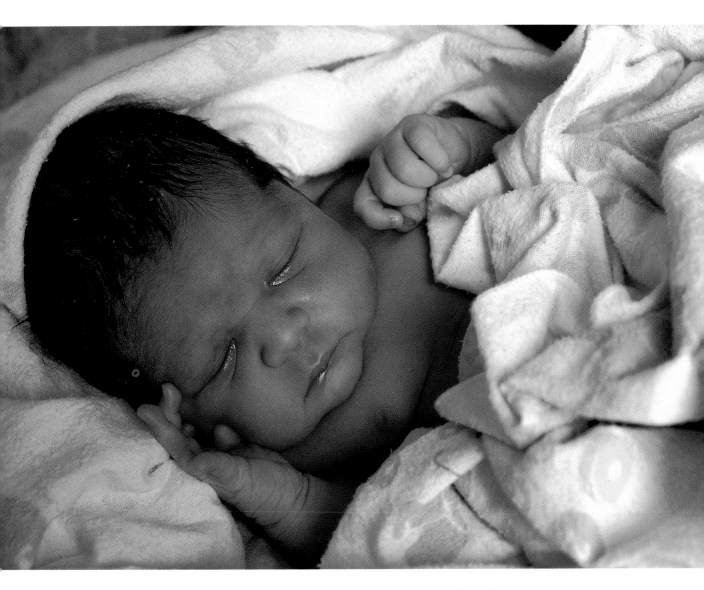

The nurse wrapped you in a blanket to keep you warm.

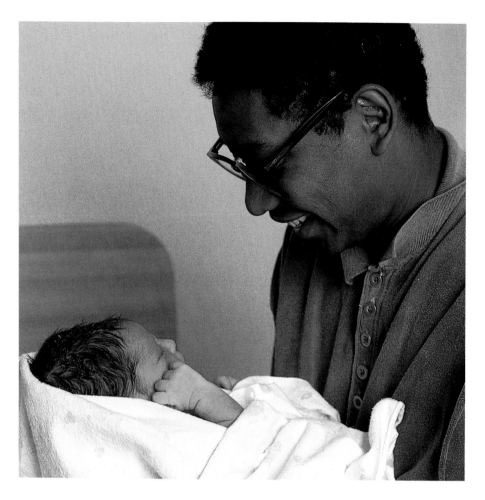

Imagine how excited and happy your
parents were when you were finally born!
Now, after months of waiting, they could
hold you in their arms and get to know
you for the first time.

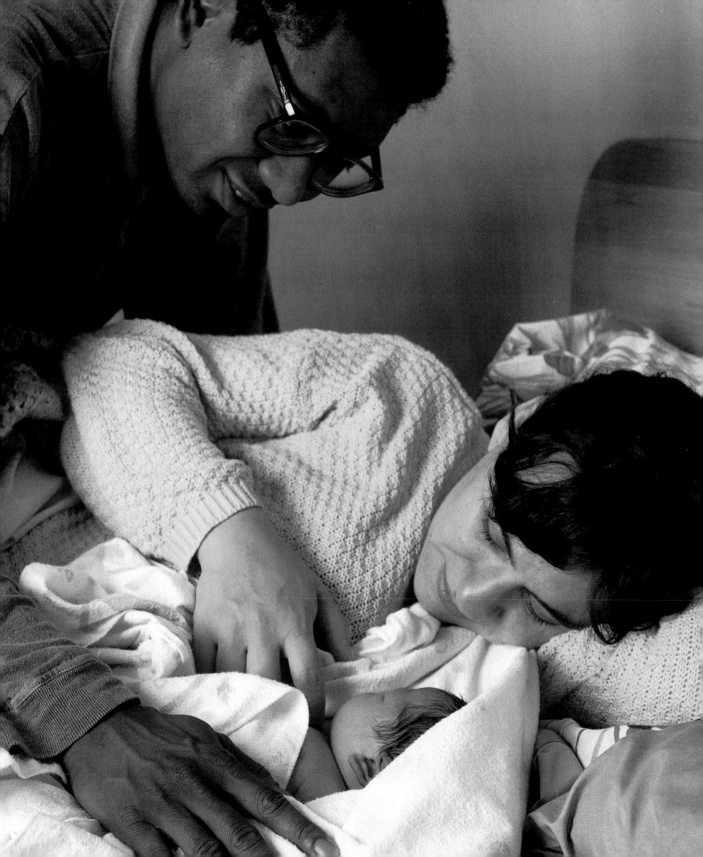

Once you were born, you could eat and breathe on your own. You didn't need the umbilical cord anymore. The doctor clamped it shut with a plastic clip and cut it. There was no feeling in the cord, so cutting it did not hurt.

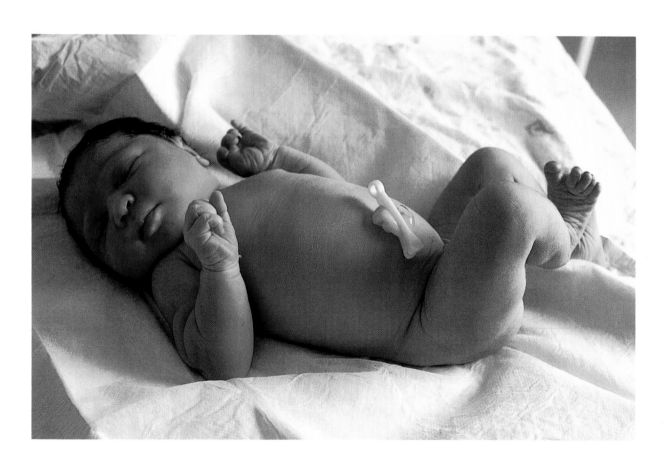

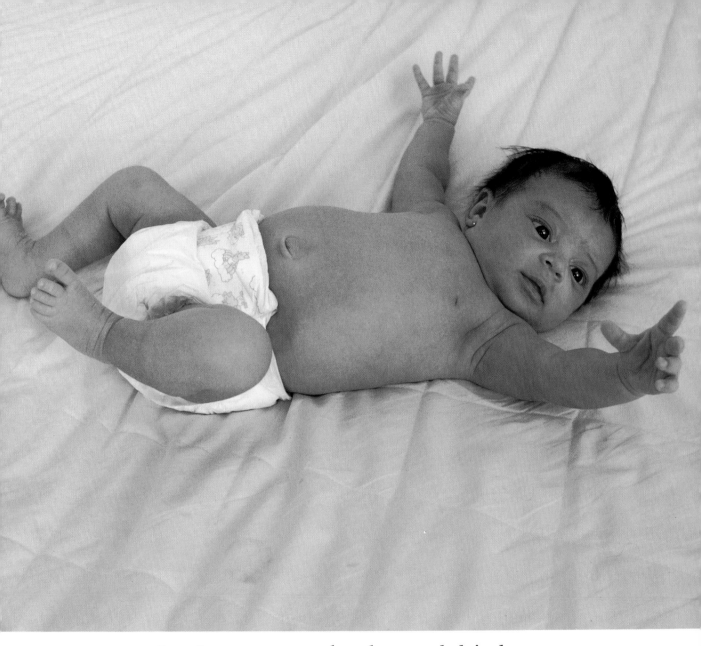

In about two weeks, the cord dried up
and fell off. The place where the cord
used to be is your navel, or belly button.

Even when you were only a few minutes old, you could see, hear, feel, taste, and smell. When your parents held you, you could see their faces clearly. When you heard a person's voice, you might turn your head toward the sound. If you were crying, you might become quiet when you felt someone holding you.

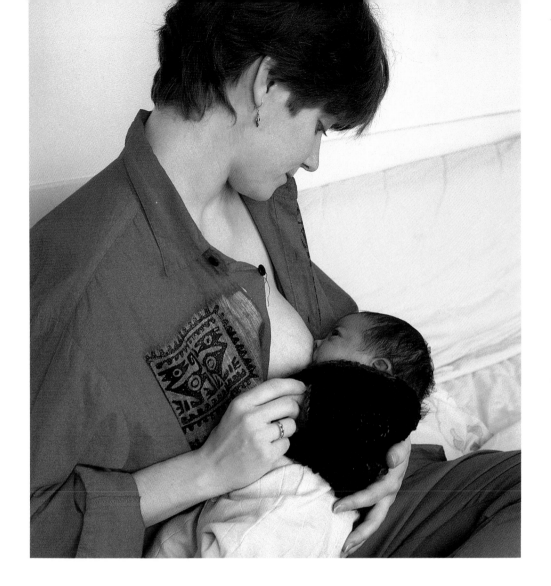

When you were hungry, you sucked milk
from your mother's breast or from a bottle.
And by the time you were a few weeks old,
you had learned to tell your mother from
other people simply by your sense of smell.

Right from the start, you noticed the people around you more than anything else. You were born ready to be part of a family, ready to learn to love and be loved.

Little by little, you learned more things: to smile and laugh, to play with toys, to crawl and walk, to babble and then say your first words. You were growing up.

Every newborn baby is the beginning of
a person—a person with feelings and
ideas who will one day build things, make
friends, and have fun. A person who can
learn all kinds of new things every day.

A person just like *you*!